Sometimes you must start from a blank slate to end confusion.

This book is dedicated to Anthony John Moore, Halle Amor Moore, Andrew Jalil Moore, & Marie Pearl Moore.

If you are reading this book you know that you need help when it comes to personal finance.

This book was written specifically to address the financial literacy need in the Black community. If you are not Black this book will still be of service to you.

The importance of smaller steps

I do not want you to work harder, I want you to work smart.

Table of Contents

Introduction

savant moore's
Cub Steps
HOW TO BECOME DEBT-FREE.

Step 00: Protect
Get Life Insurance/ Burial Policy to protect your LEGACY.

Step 0: Budget
Start a Zero-based Budget.

Step 1: Emergency Fund
Put $500 in your (fireproof + waterproof safe).

Step 2: Invest
Open a brokerage account and automate 20% of your paycheck to your wealth fund (invest in low cost index fund).

Step 3: Pay Off
Pay off debt using the LION method.

Step 4 : Save
Save 3-12 months living expenses.

Step 5: Own
Purchase/ Pay off home in 7 years.

Step 6 : Travel
Travel domestically + internationally.

Step 7 : Give
Give Black + Local

Step 8: Teach
Teach every child in your family what you learned/ what YOU do regarding financial literacy.

savant moore

By you reading through this entire book you will know everything it takes

for you to become a millionaire and change your family tree.

DO IT!

If you have heard of the Debt Free Community or FIRE (Financial Independence Retire Early) many were inspired by Dave Ramsey's 7 Baby Steps and JL Collin's Simple Path to Wealth.

I created Savant Moore's Cub Steps to fill in the missing gaps to address personal finance geared towards the plight of the Black American.

This whole journey is going to require you to have a mind shift. You are building a legacy of abundance. You will no longer say you cannot afford something. The mindset of a financial LION is imperative to be the conduit for change in your personal and family's financial picture.

This journey will take about 2-5 years, but it will be worth it.

Disclosure: Before we dive into this book, I want to make it clear that I am not a licensed real estate agent, lawyer, accountant, CPA, CFP, etc. I am not licenced in any way and I am not giving you financial advice. I am just a Black man who is going to share with you my strategy for living debt free by budgeting, saving, and investing.

Start saying this Morning Affirmations daily:

Morning Affirmations
WRITTEN BY A BLACK QUEEN: SHAW DRAKE

WHO are you?
I AM a goal crusher.

WHO can stop you from achieving your goals?
NO ONE but ME.

Are you sure?
I am sure of myself and confident in my abilities.
My potential to succeed is infinite.
I am and always will be more than enough.

What about your friends?
I surround myself with positive influences.
I teach others to believe in me by first believing in myself.

And what about your habits?
Today, I let go of old habits and create new, positive ones.

What about your mind?
My mind is powerful.

What about your heart?
My heart is happy.

What about your spirit?
My spirit is free.

Challenges will come.
Every challenge I face is an opportunity to grow and succeed.

WHAT are you?
I am a powerful creator.

WHAT do you create?
The life I want to live.

What if you fail?
I either WIN or I WIN.
I always strive for excellence again and again.
I can never fail because I will never quit.
I can never fail because I will never quit.

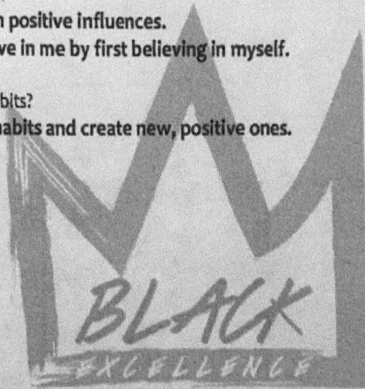

These are a few affirmations or phrases I use when I am feeling stuck in self-doubt or repeating unproductive thoughts:

- I am perfect exactly as I am.
- I am growing and becoming.
- I am enough.
- I am right where I'm supposed to be.
- I have all that I need within me now.
- I am here for a purpose.
- I love myself.
- I am here.
- I can take up space.
- I trust myself.
- I am on my own unique path.
- I trust my process.

Affirmations can be used in a variety of ways, including the following:

- Post the phrases on mirrors, fridges, or other highly visible places.
- Create screensavers or backgrounds on your phone or other devices.
- Repeat the phrase while "tapping" (Emotional Freedom Technique).
  - Write in journals or planners as part of a daily practice.
    - Create affirmation cards to pull each morning.
    - Shift the "I" to "You" and affirm your loved ones.

I hope you read this book from cover to cover and use everything it. Also let me let you in on a little secret: **You only need 1 plan to be a success story**. Do not entangle too many thought leaders on your journey towards financial freedom. Chose a path and see it through the end so that your LEGACY is not just a dream, but a reality.

Chapter 1 Cub Step 00: Protect
Get Life Insurance/Burial Policy to protect your LEGACY.

This step is more than just life insurance and a burial policy. This step is about knowing the history of Black wealth. We have tried for centuries to uplift ourselves against all odds. This book was written during a time when we have our best chance to build lasting financial wealth that can be taught on how to maintain, pass on, and keep for generations.

We have all heard the stories from post slavery, Reconstruction, Black Wall Street, redlining, systemic racist laws and everything else that has tried to stop us on our journey to build LEGACY.

This step is a safety net to help if we ever must fight against them again.

In the game of roulette, betting on either 0 or 00(if you are playing American roulette) pays out at 35/1. If you are playing American roulette and do a "row bet", this means that you are betting on either 0 or 00. If the ball falls on either 0 or 00, you will receive a 17/1 payout.

Step 00 will payout your family and they will be grateful for your wise choice.

I am tired of going to funerals funded by Go Fund Me campaigns or seeing families stuck in a financial rut because there was no preparation for the ending that happens for every human life. News flash we are all mortal and going to die. I pray that more of us die from natural causes in old ages after enjoying a long fulfilled happy life, but unfortunately that will not be the case for many. So, on the marathon of wealth building and passing on legacy for generations, it is important that we all have a life insurance and burial policy.

How Much Does a Funeral Cost? The average funeral costs between $7,000 and $12,000. This includes viewing and burial, basic service fees, transporting remains to a funeral home, a casket, embalming, and other preparation. The average cost of a funeral with cremation is $6,000 to $7,000. A burial plot on average will be $3K or a mausoleum on average will be $8K-$11K. You could be spending from $3K-$24K just on a funeral.

A funeral home will allow you to put a down payment of 10%-20% on a burial plot or mausoleum. Something we should be thinking about 30+ in age. You will have 2-4 years to pay it off.

I strongly suggest you do this. Better to be prepared than not be ready for the inevitable.

Savant Moore
@savantmoore

If you don't have life **insurance** if you have kids get it. Everyone should have a funeral expense policy.

At the writing of this book the life expectancy of
Black Americans is 72-80 years old.

The importance of the burial policy is to take finance out of mourning.
We should give our family members peace of mind by having that in order.
I encourage everyone to have a will and trust as well. Inform your
closest family members and friends how you want your funeral to be.
I know I want one of my yearly photo shoot pictures as my main
picture on the program. My favorite color is blue so have me in
a tailored blue suit. I know I want it to be a celebration,
so I want a New Orleans's second line band to play at the end.
I want to be buried in Houston, Texas a legend!

After you become wealthy you will get an irrevocable trust and
place every single family member's life insurance in it to
build generational wealth forever like the Rockefeller family did.

I want every Black family to learn from the wealthiest families in
America and start getting whole life insurance on every single
family member. This will also speed up the process of building
4 generations of wealth. These policies will allow us to have a leg up
and fund educational pursuits, entrepreneurial ideas, and just be there
in general if a family member is on hard times.

When you get life insurance Black people only get whole life insurance.
Term life insurance is cheaper because it is temporary
and has no cash value.
Whole life costs more but lasts a lifetime
and has cash value.

Get a life insurance policy for every child. The younger you are the more affordable the policy. I recommend whole life insurance only.

You are saving, investing, and becoming debt free because you are the hero of your family. On your heroic journey your protection is life insurance and a burial policy.

AMERICA'S RACIAL WEALTH GAP

$17,150 $171,000

NET WORTH OF A BLACK FAMILY   NET WORTH OF A WHITE FAMILY

BROOKINGS

DOW FUTURES
31,484.00
26.00
+0.08%

FOX BUSINESS
5:50A MT
★ BLACK HISTORY MONTH ★
IAS FUT 13,753.00 ▼14.75 -0.11% RUS2K FUT 2,267.90 ▼2.90 -0.13%

Every Black family having a life insurance policy
will help lessen this wealth gap.

Definition of legacy: 1. A gift by will especially of money or other personal property. 2. Something transmitted by or received from an ancestor or predecessor or from the past the legacy of the ancient philosophers.

What will be your legacy?

What will you leave behind?

The Cub Steps will help you answer this question.

Chapter 2 Cub Step 0: Budget

Start a Zero-based Budget.

Budget every time you get paid.

At a minimum once a month for the rest of your life.

There are 8760 hours in a year. I am only asking for you to commit to using 3 hours a year to commit to budgeting.

15 minutes the 1st of every month.

Savant Moore
@savantmoore

SIMPLE PERSONAL FINANCE:

Every time you get paid–
10% tithe/give

10% home fireproof waterproof safe to maintain 1 month living expenses

20% invest in index funds/stocks preferably FZROX, FTBFX, & SPRXX

5% fun money

10% gas/transportation

45% bills/eliminate debt

As a Christian I will always tithe every time I get paid 10% to give back to my church. If you are not a Christian, I still encourage you to give back to a local church, local charity, or Historically Black Colleges and Universities. Giving is a secret weapon to helping your finances get instantly better and you will feel good too including your tax returns.

As a realist I know the importance of having cash in case no power or phone lines. So, save 10% in your home fireproof waterproof safe.

As a human that wants to see old age, I know the importance of investing in the stock market for when that time comes to live from while I am retired. So, invest 20% in an index fund(s).

As a person that likes to have fun, I save 5% so that I can spend on whatever I want with no judgement.

As a car driver I save 10% in case of car maintenance needed.

With zero based budgeting you know where every dollar you make goes on your budget. Make sure at the end of every budget that you do for life you can do the equation Income – Expenses = $0.

Technology is great until it fails you. So, you will be using a pencil/pen and paper to write out your budget. You will pay your rent/mortgage, utilities, groceries, phone bill, insurance, clothes, debt, and miscellaneous. Every dollar will be allocated to something. Thank me later.

Chapter 3 Cub Step 1: Emergency Fund
Put $500 in your (fireproof + waterproof safe).

This step is particularly important. Too many Americans live paycheck to paycheck (69-80%) and by you building this habit of saving you will break an awfully bad habit.

$500 inside your home fireproof waterproof safe is the umbrella you need just in case of some financial rain in your life. One day that $500 will be $10-$15K. I believe in you because you are reading this book. So now all you must do is go get that $500 legally as soon as possible.

You need to purchase a fireproof waterproof safe. A safe can cost from $20-$150. Usually, the safe can last in a fire for 30 mins and submerged in water for 80hrs.

Natural disasters, emergencies, and power outages happen so this will enable you to eventually have a place to save 1 month of living expenses inside and know it is protected.

They say credit is Queen and cryptocurrency may be the future, but I know when the phone lines are down or power off, and you need to eat cash is king and will feed your family.

5 rules that guarantee success

1. Keep your higher power first
2. Treat your significant other better than yourself
3. Always have an **emergency** fund
4. Whatever your profession strive to be the best
5. Travel domestically and internationally

For now, I want you to put $500 inside your fireproof waterproof safe just in case you must replace all 4 tires on your car at once while you are paying off debt, saving, and investing.

This will give you peace of mind on your journey on each Cub Step to becoming a Debt Free LION.

If you do not have a bank account. Open a checking and savings at a credit union or bank.

People only have money on the 1st-5th or paydays then it is spent. This Cub Step needs to be done so they have money to spend.

Stop managing money for others to win check cashing places, payday loans, and living paycheck to paycheck.

Manage money for you to win with a bank/credit union with checking and savings with direct deposit, saving, and investing.

Savant Moore
@savantmoore

Save $1000 **emergency** fund by Feb 28 #BSFChallenge

Paid biweekly save $167
Weekly save $77
Monthly save $334 starting Dec. 1st

Chapter 4 Cub Step 2: Invest

***Open a brokerage account and automate 20% of your paycheck to
your wealth fund (invest in a low cost index fund)***

You can be a millionaire just by investing in 3 mutual funds, it just
takes 5-10 years. Everyone wants to be a day trader but does not have
the $25K to learn to be good at it. Everyone wants to get rich fast,
that does not exist versus guaranteed long-term investing.

You can only get rich 4 ways: High paying job, real estate, stocks,
or own a business. Stocks the easiest route,
but people do not have the patience.

**Having your investment accounts at one broker can make
them much easier to manage. I use Fidelity.**

Open a Fidelity brokerage account. Open cash management account and brokerage account. You will need to have both. You will select Core: Government. Make sure you order the Fidelity debit card attached to your new cash management account.

Investing and trading

Brokerage Account – The Fidelity Account®

Open a Brokerage Account

Brokerage and Cash Management

Open Both Accounts

Fidelity 🔒 The Fidelity Account® and Fidelity® Cash Management Account

Questions?

Open Brokerage & Cash Management Accounts

Opening a new account takes just a few minutes. Before you begin, find out what information you'll need to provide.

All fields required unless otherwise noted.

Are you already a Fidelity customer?

Yes	No

Select Yes if you have a brokerage, IRA, 401(k), or other Fidelity account

Feedback

Will this be an individual or joint account?

An individual account will only be owned by you and a joint account is one that will be shared with someone else.

Account Ownership

| Individual | Joint |

Feedback

| Next |

Exit

Money in a cash management account can usually be used to pay bills

and make purchases, sometimes with use of a debit card or check writing;

money in a brokerage account is strictly for buying, trading

and selling stocks, bonds, funds and other securities.

Savant Moore
@savantmoore

⋯

You can't **save** your way to #FIRE
You have to invest!

#FIRE: Financial Independence Retire Early

I want you to open both a brokerage and cash management account. The reason I do this is because my strategy has you growing your investments and emergency fund in the stock market. If you had an emergency bigger than 1 month of living expenses that should be in your home safe. You would have access to it with your debit card attached to your cash management account.

Simple path to wealth:

Invest by percentage.

76% = VTSAX

23% = VBTLX The Total Bond Market Index Fund.

1% = Cash in VMRXX.

A checking account at your local credit union/bank for ready cash and paying bills.

Live off 4.5% of returns a year.

You will need $2500 for initial investment in VTSAX and VBTLX each.

Savant Moore
@savantmoore

・・・

I have been telling Black people to **invest** in VTSAX for years!

Annual Total Return (%) History

Year		VTSAX	Category
2020		20.99%	15.83%
2019		30.80%	28.78%
2018		-5.17%	-6.27%
2017		21.17%	20.44%
2016		12.66%	10.37%
2015		0.39%	-1.07%
2014		12.56%	10.96%
2013		33.52%	31.50%
2012		16.38%	14.96%
2011		1.08%	-1.27%
2010		17.26%	14.01%

If you do not have the $2500 or $5K for initial investment plus $75 for fee you do have another option:

Grow each account up to $2500 until you can invest in Vanguard with Fidelity's zero fee index funds:
Invest by percentage.
76% in FZROX
23% in FTBFX
1% in SPRXX

You will break down the 20% from your budget that you are supposed to be investing into 76% 23% 1%. For example, if you had $200 a month to invest: 76% $152 invested in FZROX 23% $46 invested in FTBFX 1% $2 invested in SPRXX.

The books I suggest reading to learn about stocks:

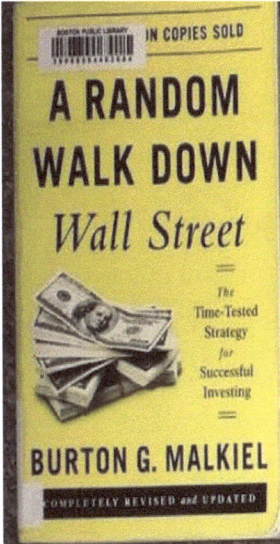

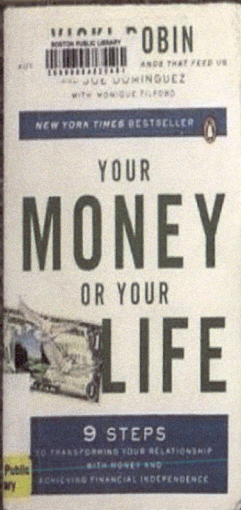

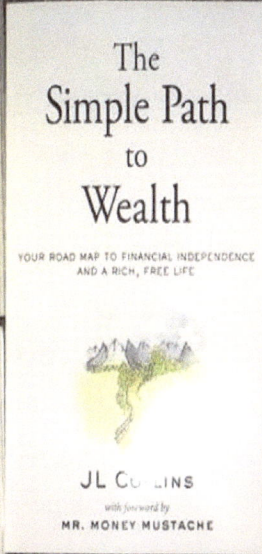

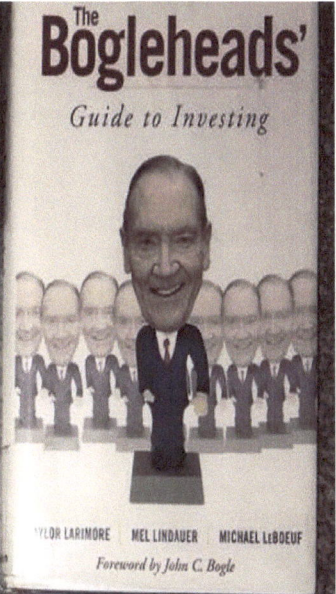

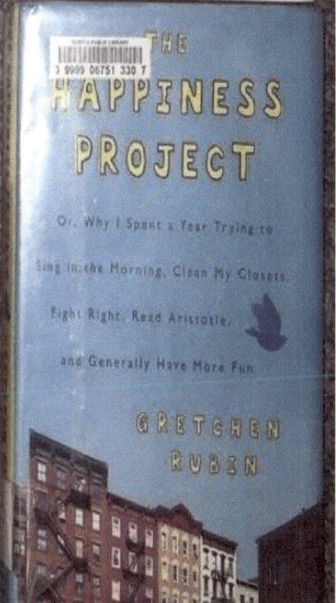

Chapter 5 Cub Step 3: Pay Off
Pay off debt using the LION™ method.

Before you read further answer these 2 questions: How much debt do you owe? What is your debt payoff date?

One strategy that I recommend that you use is the *LION™* Strategy.

First, be sure that you have budgeted enough to cover the minimum monthly payment for every debt. Now, arrange the debts by balance, from littlest to biggest. Disregard the interest rate on each.

Every month put the extra money you budgeted for getting rid of debt toward your littlest debt---even if you are paying more interest on a different one. Once the LITTLE debt is repaid, take the entire amount you were paying toward it (monthly minimum plus your extra money) and target the next-LITTLE debt. Keep knocking off debts and then diverting all the freed-up money toward the next debt in line.

Here is how it could look in real life: If you have a hospital bill for $1,200 that the hospital is allowing you to pay interest-free, and two credit card bills for $5,000 (at 22.9% interest) and $3,000 (at 15.9%), you will pay the hospital bill first. That is right ---you would pay the interest-free loan before you paid those that accrue interest. You need to front-load your payoff plan with early victories in order to stick with it, LION is for you.

LION: Little Investment Onto Next

You will make minimum payments on all your debts and focus on making extra payments on the little debt. Once paid off you will move the extra payments to another debt at a time until you have paid off all debt from little to biggest debt in full.

This little investment into yourself will help you be able to email me at smoore@dadestreet.com so I can interview you for your Debt Free Lion Roar!!!

On your journey towards paying off all your debt and becoming debt free like me. You need to get a second job and start a side business to help increase your revenue.

I used gig economy like Door Dash and Uber Eats as a second job and started side businesses from cleaning apartments to notary public.

Let all pride go and do whatever it takes legally to make your new reality of being debt free real.

Savant Moore
@savantmoore   ...

SIMPLE SMALL BUSINESS FINANCE:

40% business checking

35% pay self bi-weekly

10% business savings(portion pays quarterly taxes)

15% stay in (payment processor for any refunds) i.e. stripe

GET A SECOND JOB/START A SIDE BUSINESS SO YOU CAN PAY OFF YOUR DEBT AS SOON AS POSSIBLE! I PAID OFF $201K OF DEBT BY DOOR DASHING FOR 4 YEARS!

Chapter 6 Cub Step 4: Save

Save 3-12 months living expenses.

Storms in life will come. If you develop the habit of saving you will always be able to sleep calmly through the storm like Jesus did knowing you have the power to fix it.

80% of Americans whether rich or poor live paycheck to paycheck. I want you to be in the 20% of those that do not.

Financial health will help with mental health in our community, so we do not have to worry about finances anymore from a struggle vantage point.

Want what you want but buy what you can afford.

Emergency Fund Size Formula			
Start:	Dependents?	Industry?	Sources Of Income?
3 Months Of Fixed Costs	Yes Add 3 Months	Dying, Cyclical Add 3 Months	1 Income Add 3 Months
		Dying, Non-Cyclical Add 1 Month	2 Incomes Add 1 Month
	No Add 0 Months	Growing, Cyclical Add 1 Month	3+ Incomes Add 0 Months
		Growing, Non-Cyclical Add 0 Months	

This step is especially important. Too many Americans live paycheck to paycheck and by you building this habit of saving you will break an awfully bad habit.

Save 5-10% in a do not touch account from profits.

Entrepreneurs don't have a pension. You have to create that on your own.

We have to normalize this knowledge and use it!

Saving gives you peace of mind. Your day will go better knowing that your bank account, brokerage account, and safe has something in it. You are a long way from living paycheck to paycheck. I am immensely proud of you!

With saving being automatic and a part of your budget your whole financial picture is different. You went from a spender to a lifelong saver and investor. They say credit is Queen and Bitcoin may be the future, but I know when the phone lines are down, and you need to eat cash is king and will feed your family.

Chapter 7 Cub Step 5: Own
Purchase/Pay off home in 7 years.

You already are an investor and saver now. It is time for you to become a homeowner or pay off your home in full.

A home will most likely be your biggest purchase and it will also be one of your greatest wealth creators.

We were denied homeownership for years. Use a first-time homeowner program in your city, nonprofit NACA, USDA loan, VA loan, or FHA loan to help you become a home buyer.

Homeownership is within your reach.

Purchasing property is one of the primary ways to build wealth.

Rent is typically your highest expense, nevertheless you are paying this money to your landlord.

Invest in yourself. Buy real estate because they are not making land anymore!

You need credit to purchase a home.

Use your card and pay your balance in full monthly.

Trying to game the system is a waste of time and energy.

Focus on your complete credit profile instead of a credit score.

Generally, you want to have credit utilization under 30%.

Ideally according to FICO between 1% and 6%.

Steps to take on your journey to purchase your first home:

1. Secure your credit get all negative items removed, lower your credit to debt ratio, and broaden your credit type.

2. Chose the area you would like to move to. Decide if you want a subdivision vs a piece of land. Look at flood zones as well as drain offs. Look at city taxes and city building codes (if you decide to build something on your land after your house is built). Look at schools' types of scholarships given to students, tea recognition and testing scores. Look at the energy grid (homes near hospitals are tied into their grid so power outages are scarce). Look into home values and if they hold lower or build. If you choose a HOA ask the community for their honest thoughts on them. Use Google reviews and look at their cost. Look into what police departments and fire departments respond to your potential neighbourhood.

2. Choose the builder. Choose wisely. Look into the following: 3. incentives, materials used, reviews (5–10-year residents are best), warranty, and lastly cost.

4. Chose lender. Use mortgage choice it allows you to pick 6 lenders in the area that will compete to give you the best numbers.

5. Savings. Save at least enough to cover at least 30-45 days' worth of bills. (Important) put this money either in cash or a separate account. They monitor your accounts to

make sure you can afford your home and large amounts of money is not disappearing from your accounts during the underwriting. Also factor in furniture cost and blinds. As well as the many deposits (Cable, lights, water, gas and trash) and remember movers.

6. The big day...

I recommend asking the builder to seal the floors and counter tops some will say they are, some refuse to. Test it by dropping water in the grout if it settles it is not sealed if it beads it is. If it is not sealed seal it yourself or pay someone to before you move in. I recommend solar screens on the window but understand in emergency situations those screens will hinder your usage of them. You can also check with HOA (if you have them) to see if you can use a tint for the windows. Double check all windows and doors to make sure it is sealed.

How to pay off your mortgage in 7 years:

Ask your lender to be put on the First and 15th program for mortgage.

Pay on principal payment with a physical check and write the exact
payment for principal payment you are paying #360 and
request a new amortization schedule every time. Pay extra on
last payment forward, compound interest will be your friend. #359, #358,
#357, #356- until your mortgage is paid off.
Always request a new amortization schedule.

Use bonuses from employer and tax refunds to make extra payments.

WHAT EVERY HOME SHOULD HAVE:

Savant Moore
10m · 🌐

Advice for the young homies with their own place:

Invest in a quality mattress.

4 sleeping pillows.

300 thread count sheets

Towels restock Jan/Feb/Aug

Undershirts & underwear & socks replace every 6 months

Quality pots & pans(3-quart saucepan, 10- or 12-inch cast-iron fry pan, 10-inch nonstick fry pan, 5- or 6-quart Dutch oven, & roasting pan)

Wine glasses(6 red wine & 6 white wine)

Furniture(console table, coffee table, pouf, extra chairs, nightstand, ottoman, bedroom bench, couch, dining set, bedroom set)

Toilet paper & flushable wipes

Cleaning supplies

Laundry detergent

Food(milk, eggs, peanut butter & jelly, baking soda, variety of sauces, coffee, bread, snacks, fruits & vegetables, butter, instant dough, chicken & fish, frozen meals & snacks, grapes, ice, salt & pepper, cereal, canned goods, rice, pasta, potatoes, tuna, garlic, bananas, avocados, ramen, cooking spray) #2053project

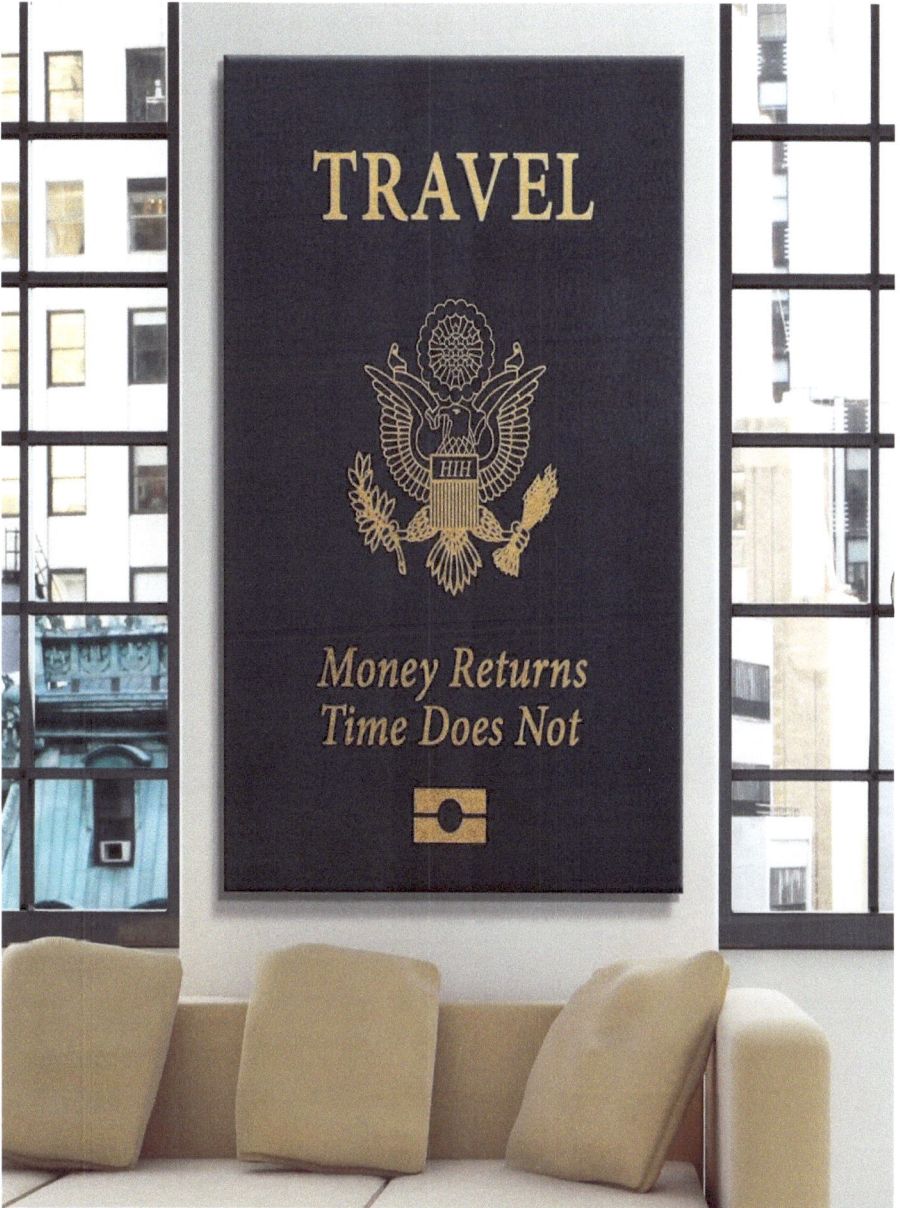

Traveling is about wealth of mind. I have taking road trips all over the country as a kid and adult. It exposed me to new worlds within my own country. New enlightening perspectives.

I have travelled all over the world as well. Get a passport and use it. My first time into Africa was jumping out of an airplane into Egypt when I was in the Army. I will never forget seeing the Nile River and pyramids up close and personal.

TSA PreCheck® costs $85 and Global Entry costs $100 for a five-year membership. Travelers interested in Global Entry must apply through the Trusted Traveler Program website. Global Entry, NEXUS, and SENTRI are programs of U.S. Customs and Border Protection.

Each is good for 5 years. Global Entry comes with TSA PreCheck® included.

Every American's goal should be to see all 50 states and the 215 countries in the world.

Traveling will expand your mind and give you exposure that will be life changing.

It will ultimately make you appreciate your home more but teach you how to respect everyone else's home.

Now that you live on a zero-based budget and know where every dollar is going you can use your fun money to see the US and world. Travel does not just include flying, if you do not know how to drive (LEARN). Also experience ATVs and water vehicles.

Historically, we used to have to use the Green Book to know where we could travel safely as a Black American.

Use this time now to see the country and all its historical landmarks. At a minimum see every capital in the US and world or at least try too.

Chapter 9 Step 7: Give
Give Black + Local.

This is especially important. You are wealthy now and you cannot spend it all. By you giving you help those in the position you may have once been in. We are all family. So be there for one another. Give back to a Black church, HBCU or local Black charity in your city.

Do not just give back for the tax benefits.
Give back because it is the right thing to do.

Whether it is the Black church, HBCU, or a local Black charity organization that is putting in long hours to serve their community, give back. They need funds in order to operate. Giving is a way of life and it is just as important as saving, investing, and home ownership.

Never forget where you came from because you may one day return.

Savant Moore
@savantmoore

I love **giving back**. Due to COVID-19 we have to be more creative. You can surprise a gig worker, homeless person, or a family you know needs the help. Give 10% monthly to causes that you're passionate about.
#LeadersDemonstrateBGE

Chapter 10 Step 8: Teach
Teach every child in your family what you learned/what YOU do regarding financial literacy.

Make sure you are having a monthly finance meeting at your home every payday. Treat your family like you are a Fortune 500 company. You are the CEO and must lead from the front when it comes to your finances.

The example you set will be followed by your family when they see you enjoying the debt free LION lifestyle.

This book was written to be put in your hands to save your immediate family. It is a numbers game. If this book can be in every Black family, we will save the collective. This should be the Christmas gift that is mandatory. This should be required reading in every grade level especially in high school. We must teach so nobody in your family ever makes a financial mistake again.

For example:

Credit is needed but we must all be responsible when using it.

Only use 7-15% credit utilization on your credit card. Pay it off in full every month. Only use it to put gas in your car, purchase airline ticket, hotel room, or rent a car.

If you are a business owner apply for your DUNS number and pay your bills on time to build up your business credit history.
Business credit only
looks at payment history.
So always pay on time within 5 days of receiving a bill.

If you are a business owner you should have a legal entity (LLC or INC), EIN number, DUNS number, business checking and savings at a credit union or Black owned bank.

Those are just examples of what you should be teaching your family.

Always remember you are wealthy and that the knowledge you now have from this book APPLY IT TO YOUR LIFE AND TEACH OTHERS THE CUB STEPS TOO SO EVERYONE CAN BE A LION.

Final Resolution

Annual Expenses	Retirement Number
$48,000	$1,200,000
$60,000	$1,500,000
$72,000	$1,800,000
$84,000	$2,100,000
$96,000	$2,400,000
$108,000	$2,700,000
$120,000	$3,000,000
$180,000	$4,500,000
$240,000	$6,000,000

Once you reach your desired retirement number you can live off the annual expenses for 25 years by withdrawing 4.5% a year from your investments.

You will divide annual expenses by 12 and that will be the amount you sell every month to live off.

You will divide annual expenses by 26 and that will be the amount you sell every month if you want to pay yourself biweekly.

You should be able to automate this with your broker.

If you follow every step you should be able to do this in 5-10 years from investing in the 2 mutual funds and 1 money market account every month consistently.

**You can do this. Eliminate all excuses and make it happen.
You are an adult and LION!**

I understand you have other obligations. But this is something you need to do. Take the time to organize your finances.
Start with Step 00.

This book was your solution. You know the problem.
No more delay to you finishing debt free and wealthy.

DEBT FREE PRAYER:

Heavenly Father,

Everyone that purchases and reads this book or finds this book
in the library, at their school, gifted it, or just reads it for free somewhere.
Bless them to use the financial knowledge to build 4 generations of
wealth for their family. Create good habits in their life for everything
financial, physical, mental, all relationships, job, and business. Let them
know they are wealthy in all aspects of their life. If they do not know
you Lord touch their mind, heart, and soul. In Jesus name. Amen.

James 1:22-24 New Living Translation
22 But don't just listen to God's word. You must do what it says.
Otherwise, you are only fooling yourselves. 23 For if you listen to the word
and don't obey, it is like glancing at your face in a mirror. 24 You see
yourself, walk away, and forget what you look like.

Savant Moore's theory to close the Black wealth gap:

Jewish use real estate to change their family tree.

Africans use college to change their family tree(doctor, lawyer, engineer).

Asians use business to change their family tree(chain of family ran businesses).

Hispanics use cash only, real estate, and small business(cleaning, lawn care, construction, trades) to change their family tree.

For Black Americans imagine if we use American businesses to change our family tree through whole life insurance like the Rockefellers and the stock market.

1st Black generation that is 16 and above- Stock market main source of income

2nd Black generation 15 and under- college/real estate via 529 as room and board and rent out rooms to other college students/stock market

3rd Black generation- Life insurance babies and get loans from life insurance to fund college and business ventures and pay back plus interest.

Every Black generation is required to have permanent whole life insurance and family LLC inside a trust.

BLACK MUST HAVES

Drink water daily

Exercise 3x's a week

Legal income (We're boycotting prisons)

Black owned bank account

Debit card(We're boycotting prepaid)

Emergency savings fund($10K)

Read 1 book a month

Drivers License(valid)

Registered voter(We vote in all elections)

Insurance(health, car, life)

Know how to swim

Passport($115 good for 10 years)

700+ credit score

CCW

Until you have everything on this list..
Why are you wasting time?
BE WOKE AND LIVE IT✊🏽

In Loving Memory
of
Rev. Harold T. Moore

The Late Pastor
of
Greater Morning Star Baptist Church
(1987-2007)

Psa. 133:1 ....Behold, how good and how pleasant it is for brethern to dwell together in unity!

Until we meet again......

REST IN POWER DAD 1945-2007

www.ingramcontent.com/pod-product-compliance
Lightning Source LLC
LaVergne TN
LVHW010029070426
835513LV00001B/27